Chapters

Chapter 1: Introduction to Effective Digital Marketing

Chapter 2: Understanding the Digital Marketing Landscape

Chapter 3: Setting Clear Campaign Objectives and Goals

Chapter 4: Targeting the Right Audience: Segmentation and Persona Development

Chapter 5: Crafting Compelling Content for Digital Channels

Chapter 6: Leveraging Social Media for Campaign Success

Chapter 7: Search Engine Optimization (SEO): Driving Organic Traffic

Chapter 8: Pay-Per-Click Advertising (PPC) Strategies

Chapter 9: Email Marketing: Nurturing Leads and Building Customer Relationships

Chapter 10: Influencer Marketing: Harnessing the Power of Digital Influencers

Chapter 11: Maximizing Conversion Rates with Landing Page Optimization

Chapter 12: Harnessing the Potential of Mobile Marketing

Chapter 13: Measuring Campaign Success: Key Metrics and Analytics

Chapter 14: A/B Testing and Optimization Techniques

Chapter 15: Building Long-Term Digital Marketing Strategies

Chapter 1: Introduction to Effective Digital Marketing

Introduction:

In today's digital age, marketing has evolved significantly, and businesses must adapt to stay competitive. This chapter serves as an introduction to effective digital marketing, providing an overview of its importance, key components, and fundamental principles.

1.1 The Digital Marketing Landscape:

This section delves into the ever-expanding digital marketing landscape, highlighting the shift from traditional marketing channels to online platforms. It explores the immense potential and reach of digital marketing, emphasizing the need for businesses to embrace it to connect with their target audiences.

1.2 Benefits of Digital Marketing:

Here, we explore the numerous benefits of digital marketing over traditional marketing methods. We discuss how digital marketing offers cost-effectiveness, targeted audience reach, measurable results, and real-time engagement. Additionally, we examine how it enables personalized experiences and facilitates data-driven decision-making.

1.3 Core Components of Digital Marketing:

This section outlines the core components of an effective digital marketing strategy. We explore key elements such as website optimization, content marketing, social media marketing, search engine marketing, email marketing, and mobile marketing. By understanding these components, readers gain a comprehensive view of the digital marketing ecosystem.

1.4 Consumer Behavior in the Digital Era:

Digital marketing is closely tied to consumer behavior and preferences. This section explores how the internet has transformed consumer decision-making and the customer journey. We discuss the importance of understanding consumer intent, online research habits, and the role of social proof in influencing purchase decisions.

1.5 Integrated Marketing Approach:

An effective digital marketing strategy integrates various channels and tactics to create a cohesive brand experience. This section emphasizes the importance of adopting an integrated marketing approach that aligns online and offline efforts. We explore how consistency across channels and touchpoints enhances brand recognition, credibility, and customer loyalty.

1.6 Key Principles of Effective Digital Marketing:

In this section, we introduce fundamental principles that underpin successful digital marketing campaigns. We cover concepts such as defining clear objectives, targeting the right audience, crafting compelling content, optimizing user experiences, measuring performance, and continuous improvement. These principles provide a solid foundation for readers to build effective digital marketing strategies.

1.7 Ethical Considerations in Digital Marketing:

Ethics play a crucial role in digital marketing. We discuss ethical considerations such as privacy, data protection, transparency, and responsible advertising. By addressing these issues, businesses can build trust and credibility with their audience, fostering long-term relationships.

1.8 The Evolution of Digital Marketing:

Digital marketing continues to evolve rapidly. In this section, we explore emerging trends and technologies shaping the future of digital marketing. Topics may include artificial intelligence, voice search, chatbots, immersive experiences, and the impact of social and cultural shifts on digital marketing strategies.

Conclusion:

This chapter concludes by summarizing the importance of effective digital marketing in today's business landscape. It reinforces the need for businesses to adapt and embrace digital channels to reach and engage their target audience effectively. By understanding the digital marketing landscape, its benefits, and key principles, readers are prepared to dive deeper into the subsequent chapters and build successful digital marketing campaigns.

Chapter 2: Understanding the Digital Marketing Landscape

Introduction:

In the rapidly evolving world of digital marketing, it is crucial for businesses to have a comprehensive understanding of the digital marketing landscape. This chapter provides an in-depth exploration of the key components, platforms, and trends that shape the digital marketing ecosystem.

2.1 The Shift to Digital Marketing:

This section outlines the reasons behind the shift from traditional marketing to digital marketing. It explores how advancements in technology, the rise of the internet, and changing consumer behaviors have created a need for businesses to embrace digital channels to reach their target audiences effectively.

2.2 Digital Marketing Channels:

Here, we delve into the various digital marketing channels available to businesses. We discuss the characteristics, advantages, and best practices for each channel, including websites, search engines, social media platforms, email marketing, content marketing, mobile apps, and online advertising. This section provides readers with a comprehensive overview of the diverse channels they can leverage in their digital marketing strategies.

2.3 Online Consumer Behavior:

Understanding consumer behavior is critical to effective digital marketing. This section explores how consumers interact with digital platforms, their online research habits, purchase decision-making processes, and the factors that influence their buying choices. By grasping the nuances of online consumer behavior, businesses can tailor their strategies to better meet their audience's needs.

2.4 Targeting and Segmentation:

Effective digital marketing relies on precise audience targeting and segmentation. This section delves into the importance of identifying target markets and breaking them down into distinct segments based on demographics, psychographics, and behavior. We discuss the benefits of personalized marketing messages and how businesses can leverage data and analytics to refine their targeting strategies.

2.5 Paid, Earned, and Owned Media:

In the digital marketing landscape, there are three main types of media: paid, earned, and owned. This section explains each category and explores how businesses can strategically leverage them. We discuss paid advertising options such as pay-per-click (**PPC**), display ads, and influencer partnerships. Earned media encompasses organic social media reach, online reviews, and public relations efforts. Lastly, owned media refers to the content businesses create on their websites, blogs, and social media profiles.

2.6 Data and Analytics:

Data plays a pivotal role in digital marketing. This section explores the importance of data collection and analysis in driving effective strategies. We discuss key metrics and analytics tools used to measure campaign performance, user behavior, website traffic, conversion rates, and more. Additionally, we touch on the ethical considerations of data collection and the importance of ensuring privacy and security.

2.7 Emerging Trends in Digital Marketing:

The digital marketing landscape is constantly evolving. In this section, we discuss emerging trends that businesses should be aware of. Topics may include voice search, artificial intelligence, chatbots, virtual reality, augmented reality, and the impact of social media and influencer marketing. By staying informed about these trends, businesses can adapt and stay ahead of the competition.

Conclusion:

This chapter concludes by summarizing the importance of understanding the digital marketing landscape. By comprehending the diverse channels, consumer behavior, targeting strategies, media types, and emerging trends, businesses can make informed decisions and develop effective digital marketing campaigns. The subsequent chapters will delve deeper into specific channels and tactics, equipping readers with practical knowledge and tools for success in the digital marketing realm.

Chapter 3: Setting Clear Campaign Objectives and Goals

Introduction:

Before embarking on a digital marketing campaign, it is essential to establish clear objectives and goals. This chapter explores the importance of setting specific, measurable, attainable, relevant, and time-bound (SMART) objectives and provides a step-by-step guide to defining goals that align with business objectives.

3.1 The Significance of Clear Campaign Objectives:

This section emphasizes the importance of setting clear campaign objectives. It discusses how well-defined objectives provide focus, direction, and a framework for measuring success. By establishing specific goals, businesses can align their digital marketing efforts with broader organizational objectives.

3.2 SMART Goal Framework:

The SMART goal framework provides a structured approach to goal setting. This section explores each element of SMART—specific, measurable, attainable, relevant, and time-bound—and how they contribute to setting effective campaign objectives. It highlights the need for objectives that are specific, quantifiable, realistic, aligned with business objectives, and bound by a clear timeline.

3.3 Defining Key Performance Indicators (KPIs):

To measure campaign success, it is crucial to identify and define key performance indicators (KPIs). This section discusses various KPIs applicable to different digital marketing channels and campaign objectives. It includes metrics such as website traffic, conversions, click-through rates, engagement, social media followers, and customer acquisition costs. By selecting relevant KPIs, businesses can monitor progress and evaluate the effectiveness of their campaigns.

3.4 Aligning Objectives with Target Audience and Segmentation:

To ensure campaign success, objectives must be aligned with the target audience and segmentation. This section explores how businesses can consider their audience's preferences, behaviors, and demographics when setting campaign objectives. It emphasizes the need to tailor objectives to resonate with the target audience and generate meaningful engagement.

3.5 Prioritizing Primary and Secondary Objectives:

Not all campaign objectives carry equal weight. This section discusses the importance of prioritizing primary and secondary objectives based on their impact on business outcomes. It provides guidance on determining the primary objective that aligns with the core purpose of the campaign while identifying supporting secondary objectives that contribute to the overall success.

3.6 Establishing Benchmark and Baseline Metrics:

To gauge campaign performance accurately, it is essential to establish benchmark and baseline metrics. This section explores the process of analyzing historical data, industry benchmarks, and competitor performance to set realistic targets and establish a starting point for measuring success. It emphasizes the need to regularly monitor and adjust goals as the campaign progresses.

3.7 Flexibility and Adaptability:

In the dynamic digital landscape, it is crucial to maintain flexibility and adaptability when setting campaign objectives. This section discusses the importance of periodically reviewing and revising objectives to align with changing market conditions, audience preferences, and emerging trends. It highlights the benefits of agility and responsiveness in optimizing campaign performance.

3.8 Communicating Objectives and Gaining Stakeholder Buy-In:

Setting clear campaign objectives requires effective communication and gaining stakeholder buy-in. This section explores strategies for effectively conveying objectives to internal teams, clients, or stakeholders. It emphasizes the importance of collaboration, shared understanding, and a sense of ownership to ensure everyone is aligned and committed to achieving the set goals.

Conclusion:

This chapter concludes by emphasizing the significance of setting clear campaign objectives and goals. By following the SMART framework, defining relevant KPIs, aligning objectives with the target audience, and fostering flexibility and adaptability, businesses can establish a solid foundation for their digital marketing campaigns. The subsequent chapters will delve into specific strategies and tactics to help achieve these objectives effectively.

Chapter 4: Targeting the Right Audience: Segmentation and Persona Development

Introduction:

Successful digital marketing campaigns rely on effectively targeting the right audience. This chapter explores the importance of audience segmentation and persona development in optimizing campaign performance. It provides insights and strategies for identifying and understanding target audiences to deliver personalized and impactful marketing messages.

4.1 The Significance of Audience Targeting:

This section highlights the critical role of audience targeting in digital marketing. It discusses how targeting the right audience enhances campaign effectiveness, improves conversion rates, and maximizes return on investment. By focusing resources on the most relevant audience segments, businesses can achieve better results and generate meaningful engagement.

4.2 Audience Segmentation:

Audience segmentation involves dividing a larger target market into distinct groups based on shared characteristics, preferences, behaviors, or demographics. This section explores different segmentation strategies, including demographic, psychographic, geographic, and behavioral segmentation. It emphasizes the importance of tailoring marketing efforts to specific segments to increase relevancy and resonance.

4.3 Developing Customer Personas:

Customer personas provide a detailed representation of target audience segments, enabling businesses to create personalized and targeted marketing campaigns. This section guides readers through the process of developing customer personas, including conducting research, gathering data, and creating fictional profiles that capture the characteristics, motivations, and pain points of different audience segments.

4.4 Data-Driven Audience Insights:

Data plays a pivotal role in audience targeting. This section discusses the use of data and analytics to gain valuable insights into audience behaviors, preferences, and needs. It explores various data sources, including website analytics, social media analytics, customer surveys, and market research. By leveraging data-driven insights, businesses can make informed decisions and refine their targeting strategies.

4.5 Understanding User Intent:

User intent refers to the underlying motivation or purpose behind a user's online activities. This section explores how understanding user intent helps businesses deliver relevant and personalized marketing messages. It covers different types of user intent, such as informational, navigational, and transactional, and provides strategies for aligning content and marketing efforts with user intent at each stage of the customer journey.

4.6 Tailoring Marketing Messages:

Effective audience targeting requires tailoring marketing messages to resonate with specific audience segments. This section explores strategies for crafting compelling and personalized content that speaks directly to the needs, interests, and pain points of different personas. It discusses the power of storytelling, emotional appeal, and addressing unique value propositions to capture audience attention and drive engagement.

4.7 Testing and Refining Audience Segments:

Audience segmentation is an iterative process. This section discusses the importance of testing and refining audience segments based on campaign performance and feedback. It explores A/B testing, user feedback, and continuous data analysis as tools for optimizing audience targeting and persona development. By refining segments over time, businesses can stay relevant and adapt to changing market dynamics.

4.8 Ethical Considerations in Audience Targeting:

Ethics play a crucial role in audience targeting. This section explores ethical considerations such as data privacy, transparency, and responsible use of personal information. It emphasizes the need to prioritize consumer trust and consent, and to adhere to legal and industry guidelines when collecting and using data for audience targeting purposes.

Conclusion:

This chapter concludes by highlighting the importance of targeting the right audience through segmentation and persona development. By understanding audience characteristics, needs, and preferences, businesses can deliver personalized marketing messages that resonate with their target customers. The subsequent chapters will delve into specific digital marketing strategies and tactics that align with effective audience targeting.

Chapter 5: Crafting Compelling Content for Digital Channels

Introduction:

In the digital marketing landscape, content serves as the backbone of engaging and impactful campaigns. This chapter explores the art of crafting compelling content that resonates with the target audience across various digital channels. It provides insights and strategies to create content that captures attention, drives engagement, and delivers results.

5.1 The Importance of Compelling Content:

This section emphasizes the critical role of compelling content in digital marketing. It discusses how well-crafted content helps businesses establish brand authority, build trust, and create meaningful connections with their audience. By delivering valuable and engaging content, businesses can attract and retain their target customers.

5.2 Understanding Audience Needs and Preferences:

Effective content begins with a deep understanding of audience needs and preferences. This section explores strategies for conducting audience research, analyzing data, and gaining insights into what motivates and interests the target audience. By understanding their pain points, aspirations, and communication preferences, businesses can tailor content to resonate with their audience.

5.3 Defining Content Objectives:

Before creating content, it is crucial to define clear objectives. This section guides readers through the process of setting content objectives aligned with broader campaign goals. It explores different content objectives, such as brand awareness, lead generation, customer education, or driving conversions. Well-defined objectives ensure that content is purposeful and drives desired outcomes.

5.4 Tailoring Content for Different Digital Channels:

Different digital channels require content to be tailored to their unique characteristics and user expectations. This section explores strategies for adapting content to various channels, such as websites, blogs, social media, email marketing, video platforms, and podcasts. It discusses considerations like format, tone, length, and interactivity to maximize content effectiveness.

5.5 The Power of Storytelling:

Storytelling is a powerful tool for creating engaging content. This section delves into the art of storytelling and its impact on capturing audience attention and building emotional connections. It explores narrative structures, compelling storytelling elements, and techniques for using storytelling to convey brand messages effectively.

5.6 Incorporating Visual and Interactive Elements:

Visual and interactive elements can enhance content engagement and convey messages effectively. This section explores the importance of incorporating visuals such as images, infographics, videos, and interactive elements like quizzes, polls, and surveys. It provides tips for creating visually appealing and interactive content that grabs attention and encourages user participation.

5.7 SEO and Content Optimization:

Search engine optimization (SEO) plays a crucial role in content visibility and organic reach. This section discusses the fundamentals of SEO and how to optimize content for search engines. It covers keyword research, on-page optimization, meta tags, link building, and the importance of providing valuable, high-quality content that meets search intent.

5.8 Creating Compelling Calls-to-Action (CTAs):

A compelling call-to-action (CTA) prompts users to take desired actions. This section explores strategies for creating persuasive CTAs that drive conversions. It discusses the importance of clear and action-oriented language, strategic placement, and the use of urgency or incentives to motivate users to take the next step.

5.9 Content Distribution and Promotion:

Creating great content is only part of the equation; effective distribution and promotion are equally important. This section explores strategies for content distribution, including social media promotion, email marketing, influencer partnerships, and content syndication. It emphasizes the need to leverage multiple channels to reach the target audience effectively.

5.10 Measuring Content Performance:

Measuring content performance is essential for evaluating effectiveness and making data-driven improvements. This section discusses key metrics and tools for measuring content performance, including website analytics, social media insights, and engagement metrics. By analyzing data and feedback, businesses can optimize content and enhance its impact.

Conclusion:

This chapter concludes by highlighting the significance of crafting compelling content for digital channels. By understanding audience needs, setting clear objectives, tailoring content for different channels, incorporating storytelling and visual elements, optimizing for search engines, creating persuasive CTAs, and effectively promoting content, businesses can create engaging content that resonates with their target audience. The subsequent chapters will delve into specific digital marketing strategies and tactics to complement content creation efforts.

Chapter 6: Leveraging Social Media for Campaign Success

Introduction:

Social media has become an integral part of digital marketing, offering businesses vast opportunities to connect with their target audience and drive campaign success. This chapter explores the strategies and best practices for leveraging social media platforms effectively. It provides insights into audience targeting, content creation, community engagement, and measurement to maximize the impact of social media campaigns.

6.1 The Power of Social Media in Digital Marketing:

This section highlights the significance of social media platforms in reaching and engaging target audiences. It discusses the widespread usage of social media, its impact on consumer behavior, and the opportunities it presents for businesses to build brand awareness, drive website traffic, generate leads, and foster customer loyalty.

6.2 Selecting the Right Social Media Platforms:

Choosing the right social media platforms is crucial for campaign success. This section explores popular social media platforms such as Facebook, Instagram, Twitter, LinkedIn, YouTube, and TikTok. It discusses the demographics, user behavior, and unique features of each platform, helping businesses make informed decisions about where to focus their social media efforts.

6.3 Defining Social Media Objectives:

Setting clear social media objectives is essential for campaign effectiveness. This section guides readers through the process of defining objectives that align with overall marketing goals. It explores objectives like increasing brand awareness, driving website traffic, boosting engagement, generating leads, nurturing customer relationships, or facilitating sales. Well-defined objectives provide direction and measurement benchmarks.

6.4 Audience Targeting and Segmentation:

Audience targeting and segmentation play a crucial role in social media campaigns. This section discusses strategies for identifying and understanding the target audience on social media platforms. It explores options for demographic targeting, interest-based targeting, and remarketing to reach the most relevant users. By segmenting the audience, businesses can tailor content and messages to specific groups for better engagement.

6.5 Creating Engaging Social Media Content:

Compelling content is key to social media success. This section delves into content creation strategies for social media platforms. It covers different content formats, including text posts, images, videos, live streaming, stories, and user-generated content. It emphasizes the need for visually appealing, informative, entertaining, and shareable content that aligns with audience preferences and platform best practices.

6.6 Fostering Community Engagement:

Engaging with the social media community is vital for building relationships and driving campaign success. This section explores strategies for fostering community engagement, such as responding to comments, asking questions, running contests or giveaways, hosting live sessions, and participating in relevant discussions. It highlights the importance of building a two-way conversation with followers and establishing a sense of community.

6.7 Influencer Marketing:

Influencer marketing has gained prominence on social media platforms. This section discusses the benefits of collaborating with influencers to amplify reach and engage the target audience. It explores strategies for identifying and partnering with influencers, establishing authentic relationships, and aligning influencer content with campaign objectives. It also highlights the importance of transparency and selecting influencers relevant to the brand and target audience.

6.8 Social Media Advertising:

Paid social media advertising can significantly enhance campaign reach and engagement. This section explores various social media advertising options, including boosted posts, sponsored content, display ads, and influencer collaborations. It discusses targeting options, ad formats, budgeting, and tracking metrics to optimize advertising campaigns on social media platforms.

6.9 Social Media Listening and Monitoring:

Social media listening and monitoring are essential for understanding audience sentiment, tracking brand mentions, and gathering insights for campaign improvement. This section explores tools and techniques for monitoring social media conversations, tracking hashtags, analyzing competitor activity, and responding to customer feedback. It emphasizes the role of data-driven insights in refining social media strategies.

6.10 Measuring Social Media Performance:

Measuring social media performance is critical for evaluating campaign success and making data-driven decisions. This section discusses key metrics and tools for measuring social media performance, including reach, engagement, clicks, conversions, and sentiment analysis. It explores analytics platforms provided by social media platforms and third-party tools for comprehensive performance tracking.

Conclusion:

This chapter concludes by highlighting the significance of leveraging social media platforms for campaign success. By selecting the right platforms, defining clear objectives, targeting the audience effectively, creating engaging content, fostering community engagement, utilizing influencer marketing, leveraging social media advertising, listening and monitoring social media conversations, and measuring performance, businesses can optimize their social media campaigns and drive tangible results.

Chapter 7: Search Engine Optimization (SEO): Driving Organic Traffic

Introduction:

In the digital landscape, search engine optimization (SEO) is a fundamental strategy for driving organic traffic to websites and increasing online visibility. This chapter explores the importance of SEO in digital marketing and provides insights and strategies for optimizing websites to rank higher in search engine results. It covers keyword research, on-page optimization, technical SEO, link building, and measurement to help businesses maximize their organic search presence.

7.1 Understanding the Importance of SEO:

This section highlights the significance of SEO in digital marketing. It explains how search engines serve as gateways to information, products, and services, making it crucial for businesses to optimize their websites to rank higher in search results. It discusses the impact of organic search traffic on brand visibility, credibility, and long-term success.

7.2 Conducting Keyword Research:

Keyword research is the foundation of effective SEO. This section explores strategies and tools for identifying relevant keywords and phrases that align with the target audience's search intent. It covers factors like search volume, competition, and keyword relevance to guide businesses in selecting the right keywords to target in their content and optimization efforts.

7.3 On-Page Optimization:

On-page optimization involves optimizing various elements on a website to improve its search engine visibility. This section discusses best practices for on-page optimization, including optimizing title tags, meta descriptions, heading tags, URL structures, and content. It emphasizes the importance of creating high-quality, relevant, and keyword-rich content that provides value to users and aligns with search engine guidelines.

7.4 Technical SEO:

Technical SEO focuses on optimizing the technical aspects of a website to enhance its search engine crawlability and indexability. This section explores technical SEO elements, such as website speed optimization, mobile responsiveness, XML sitemaps, robots.txt, canonical tags, and structured data markup. It discusses the role of technical SEO in improving user experience and search engine rankings.

7.5 User Experience and SEO:

User experience (UX) plays a vital role in SEO. This section discusses the correlation between UX and search engine rankings. It explores strategies for improving website usability, navigation, page load times, mobile optimization, and overall user satisfaction. By providing a seamless and engaging user experience, businesses can enhance their organic search performance.

7.6 Link Building:

Link building is an essential component of SEO, as it helps search engines determine a website's authority and relevance. This section explores strategies for building high-quality and authoritative backlinks, such as guest blogging, influencer partnerships, content promotion, and leveraging social media. It emphasizes the importance of earning natural, relevant, and diverse backlinks to enhance search engine rankings.

7.7 Local SEO:

Local SEO focuses on optimizing websites to rank higher in local search results. This section discusses strategies for local SEO, including optimizing Google My Business listings, obtaining online reviews, utilizing local keywords, and creating location-specific content. It explores the significance of local SEO for businesses with physical locations or those targeting specific geographic areas.

7.8 SEO Measurement and Analysis:

Measuring and analyzing SEO performance is essential for refining strategies and making data-driven decisions. This section discusses key metrics and tools for measuring SEO success, such as organic traffic, keyword rankings, click-through rates (CTRs), bounce rates, and conversion rates. It emphasizes the use of analytics platforms and SEO tools to gain insights into website performance and identify areas for improvement.

7.9 Keeping Up with SEO Trends and Updates:

SEO is a dynamic field, with search engine algorithms constantly evolving. This section explores the importance of staying updated with SEO trends, algorithm changes, and industry best practices. It discusses resources for staying informed, participating in SEO communities, and adapting strategies to align with the latest developments in search engine optimization.

Conclusion:

This chapter concludes by highlighting the crucial role of SEO in driving organic traffic to websites. By conducting keyword research, implementing on-page optimization techniques, optimizing the technical aspects of a website, building high-quality backlinks, focusing on user experience, incorporating local SEO strategies, and measuring SEO performance, businesses can improve their search engine rankings and attract valuable organic traffic.

Chapter 8: Pay-Per-Click Advertising (PPC) Strategies

Introduction:

Pay-Per-Click advertising (PPC) is a powerful digital marketing strategy that allows businesses to drive targeted traffic to their websites by paying for each click on their ads. This chapter explores the key concepts and strategies behind PPC advertising. It covers platforms, campaign setup, keyword research, ad creation, bid management, tracking, and optimization techniques to help businesses maximize their PPC campaign's effectiveness.

8.1 Understanding Pay-Per-Click Advertising:

This section provides an overview of PPC advertising and its significance in the digital marketing landscape. It explains the concept of advertisers paying for each click on their ads, the role of search engines and advertising platforms, and the benefits of PPC advertising in terms of immediate visibility, precise targeting, and measurable results.

8.2 Selecting the Right PPC Platforms:

Choosing the right PPC platforms is crucial for campaign success. This section explores popular PPC platforms such as Google Ads (formerly AdWords), Bing Ads, and social media advertising platforms like Facebook Ads and LinkedIn Ads. It discusses the unique features, audience reach, and targeting options of each platform to help businesses make informed decisions about their PPC advertising channels.

8.3 Campaign Setup and Structure:

Effective campaign setup and structure are vital for PPC success. This section delves into the process of creating PPC campaigns, including setting up accounts, defining campaign goals, structuring ad groups, and configuring campaign settings. It emphasizes the importance of aligning campaign structure with business objectives and organizing ad groups for better targeting and control.

8.4 Keyword Research and Selection:

Keyword research is a critical aspect of PPC advertising. This section explores strategies and tools for conducting keyword research to identify relevant and high-performing keywords. It discusses factors like search volume, keyword competition, and relevance to guide businesses in selecting the right keywords for their PPC campaigns. It also emphasizes the importance of negative keyword research to optimize targeting.

8.5 Ad Creation and Optimization:

Compelling ad creatives are essential to drive clicks and conversions in PPC campaigns. This section provides insights into creating effective PPC ads, including writing engaging ad copy, utilizing ad extensions, creating compelling calls-to-action (CTAs), and incorporating relevant keywords. It emphasizes the importance of testing ad variations and optimizing ad performance through continuous monitoring and refinement.

8.6 Bid Management and Budgeting:

Managing bids effectively is crucial to optimize PPC campaign performance. This section explores bid management strategies, including manual bidding, automated bidding, bid adjustments, and budget allocation. It discusses factors like keyword competitiveness, ad quality, and conversion tracking to help businesses set appropriate bids and budgets for their PPC campaigns.

8.7 Ad Targeting and Audience Segmentation:

Precise ad targeting and audience segmentation are key to maximizing the effectiveness of PPC campaigns. This section discusses targeting options such as location targeting, device targeting, demographic targeting, and audience targeting based on interests or behaviors. It explores strategies for segmenting audiences and creating tailored ad campaigns to reach the most relevant audience segments.

8.8 Conversion Tracking and Measurement:

Measuring and tracking conversions is essential for evaluating the success of PPC campaigns. This section discusses the importance of implementing conversion tracking codes and utilizing analytics platforms to measure key metrics like click-through rates (CTRs), conversion rates, and return on ad spend (ROAS). It emphasizes the role of data-driven insights in optimizing PPC campaign performance.

8.9 A/B Testing and Optimization:

A/B testing is a valuable technique for optimizing PPC campaigns. This section explores A/B testing strategies for ad creatives, landing pages, and call-to-action (CTA) buttons. It discusses testing variables such as headlines, images, ad copy, and landing page elements to identify the most effective combinations and improve campaign performance over time.

8.10 Remarketing and Display Advertising:

Remarketing and display advertising are powerful strategies to re-engage website visitors and target audiences beyond search results. This section discusses remarketing techniques, display ad creation, and audience targeting options to maximize the impact of these campaigns. It explores the use of banner ads, responsive ads, and video ads to reach and convert potential customers.

Conclusion:

This chapter concludes by highlighting the significance of PPC advertising as a targeted and measurable strategy to drive traffic and conversions. By selecting the right PPC platforms, conducting thorough keyword research, creating compelling ads, managing bids effectively, optimizing campaigns through testing and tracking, and leveraging remarketing and display advertising, businesses can achieve successful PPC campaigns that deliver tangible results.

Chapter 9: Email Marketing: Nurturing Leads and Building Customer Relationships

Introduction:

Email marketing remains one of the most effective digital marketing strategies for nurturing leads, building customer relationships, and driving conversions. This chapter explores the power of email marketing and provides insights into best practices for creating engaging email campaigns. It covers list building, segmentation, email design, personalization, automation, testing, and measurement to help businesses leverage email marketing for success.

9.1 The Importance of Email Marketing:

This section highlights the significance of email marketing in the digital marketing landscape. It discusses the high ROI, widespread use, and direct communication opportunities that email marketing offers. It emphasizes the role of email campaigns in nurturing leads, building trust, driving conversions, and fostering long-term customer relationships.

9.2 Building and Growing an Email List:

A strong and engaged email list is crucial for successful email marketing. This section explores strategies for building and growing an email list, including website opt-in forms, lead magnets, gated content, social media promotions, and offline events. It emphasizes the importance of obtaining permission and providing value to subscribers to encourage sign-ups.

9.3 Email Segmentation and Personalization:

Segmentation and personalization are key components of effective email marketing. This section discusses strategies for segmenting email lists based on demographics, behavior, interests, or engagement levels. It explores the benefits of personalized email content, such as targeted messaging, dynamic content, and personalized product recommendations, to improve engagement and conversions.

9.4 Creating Engaging Email Content:

Compelling email content is essential to capture the attention of subscribers and drive engagement. This section explores strategies for creating engaging email content, including attention-grabbing subject lines, concise and scannable copy, visually appealing designs, and clear call-to-action (CTA) buttons. It emphasizes the importance of providing value, delivering relevant information, and using storytelling techniques to engage readers.

9.5 Email Automation and Drip Campaigns:

Email automation allows businesses to deliver targeted and timely messages to subscribers based on their behavior or predefined triggers. This section explores email automation and drip campaigns, including welcome emails, abandoned cart emails, re-engagement emails, and customer onboarding sequences. It discusses the benefits of automation in saving time, improving customer experience, and nurturing leads.

9.6 Testing and Optimization:

Testing and optimizing email campaigns are essential for improving their effectiveness. This section discusses A/B testing strategies for subject lines, email content, CTAs, and design elements. It explores metrics such as open rates, click-through rates (CTRs), and conversion rates to measure the performance of email campaigns and make data-driven improvements.

9.7 Email Deliverability and Compliance:

Ensuring email deliverability and compliance with anti-spam regulations is critical for successful email marketing. This section explores best practices for maintaining a good sender reputation, including using reputable email service providers (ESPs), avoiding spam triggers, implementing double opt-in processes, and including clear unsubscribe options. It emphasizes the importance of adhering to email marketing regulations and respecting subscribers' preferences.

9.8 Email Analytics and Measurement:

Measuring the success of email campaigns is essential for refining strategies and optimizing results. This section discusses key email marketing metrics, including open rates, CTRs, conversion rates, and subscriber engagement. It explores email analytics platforms and tracking tools to gain insights into campaign performance and subscriber behavior.

9.9 Email Marketing for Customer Retention:

Email marketing is not just for lead nurturing but also for customer retention and loyalty. This section explores strategies for utilizing email marketing to maintain relationships with existing customers, such as personalized offers, loyalty programs, customer surveys, and exclusive content. It emphasizes the role of email communication in fostering long-term customer loyalty.

9.10 Integration with CRM and Marketing Automation:

Integrating email marketing with customer relationship management (CRM) systems and marketing automation platforms enhances the effectiveness of campaigns. This section discusses the benefits of integrating email marketing with CRM and automation tools to streamline processes, improve segmentation, and deliver targeted messaging based on customer data.

Conclusion:

This chapter concludes by highlighting the power of email marketing in nurturing leads, building customer relationships, and driving conversions. By focusing on list building, segmentation, personalization, engaging content creation, automation, testing, and measurement, businesses can leverage email marketing to foster customer loyalty and achieve marketing success.

Chapter 10: Influencer Marketing: Harnessing the Power of Digital Influencers

Introduction:

Influencer marketing has emerged as a highly effective strategy for brands to reach their target audience, build credibility, and drive engagement. This chapter explores the concept of influencer marketing and provides insights into leveraging the power of digital influencers. It covers identifying the right influencers, building relationships, campaign strategies, measurement, and best practices to help businesses harness the potential of influencer marketing.

10.1 Understanding Influencer Marketing:

This section introduces the concept of influencer marketing and its significance in the digital landscape. It explains how influencers, who have established credibility and a loyal following in specific niches, can help brands reach and engage their target audience effectively. It discusses the benefits of influencer marketing, such as increased brand awareness, social proof, and authentic content creation.

10.2 Identifying the Right Influencers:

Finding the right influencers for your brand is crucial for successful influencer marketing campaigns. This section explores strategies for identifying relevant influencers based on factors like niche alignment, audience demographics, engagement rates, and authenticity. It discusses tools and platforms that can assist in influencer discovery and evaluation.

10.3 Building Relationships with Influencers:

Building strong relationships with influencers is essential for effective collaboration and campaign success. This section delves into the process of engaging with influencers, establishing rapport, and nurturing mutually beneficial partnerships. It discusses approaches such as personalized outreach, providing value to influencers, and fostering long-term relationships.

10.4 Campaign Strategies and Execution:

Executing influencer marketing campaigns requires careful planning and collaboration. This section explores different campaign strategies, such as sponsored content, product reviews, giveaways, and influencer takeovers. It discusses the importance of aligning campaign objectives with influencer selection, setting clear expectations, and ensuring proper disclosure and transparency.

10.5 Authentic Content Creation:

Authenticity is a key aspect of influencer marketing. This section explores strategies for promoting authentic content creation by influencers. It discusses the importance of allowing influencers creative freedom, maintaining brand guidelines, and encouraging storytelling to resonate with the influencer's audience. It also emphasizes the role of user-generated content (UGC) in influencer campaigns.

10.6 Tracking and Measurement:

Measuring the impact and success of influencer marketing campaigns is crucial for evaluating return on investment (ROI). This section discusses key metrics and tracking methods for measuring the performance of influencer campaigns, such as reach, engagement, traffic, conversions, and brand sentiment. It explores tools and platforms that can assist in tracking influencer performance and campaign outcomes.

10.7 Compliance and Disclosure:

Compliance with advertising regulations and disclosure guidelines is essential in influencer marketing. This section explores the importance of transparent and compliant influencer collaborations. It discusses the guidelines set forth by regulatory bodies and platforms regarding proper disclosure of sponsored content. It emphasizes the responsibility of brands and influencers to adhere to these guidelines.

10.8 Building Long-Term Partnerships:

Long-term partnerships with influencers can yield significant benefits for brands. This section discusses the advantages of building ongoing relationships with influencers, such as consistency, brand loyalty, and extended reach. It explores strategies for nurturing long-term partnerships, including exclusive collaborations, ambassador programs, and continuous engagement.

10.9 Influencer Crisis Management:

Influencer marketing can occasionally face challenges, including influencer controversies or negative brand associations. This section explores strategies for handling influencer crises effectively. It discusses the importance of proactive communication, assessing the impact, and taking appropriate actions to mitigate any potential reputational damage.

10.10 Emerging Trends in Influencer Marketing:

Influencer marketing is an evolving field with emerging trends and strategies. This section highlights current and future trends, such as micro-influencers, nano-influencers, video content, live streaming, and influencer-generated products. It encourages businesses to stay updated with the latest trends to maximize the impact of influencer marketing.

Conclusion:

This chapter concludes by emphasizing the power of influencer marketing in reaching and engaging target audiences. By identifying the right influencers, building strong relationships, executing well-planned campaigns, tracking performance, and adapting to emerging trends, businesses can harness the potential of influencer marketing to achieve their marketing goals.

Chapter 11: Maximizing Conversion Rates with Landing Page Optimization

Introduction:

Landing page optimization plays a crucial role in driving conversions and maximizing the effectiveness of digital marketing campaigns. This chapter explores the key principles and strategies behind landing page optimization. It covers design elements, persuasive copywriting, call-to-action (CTA) optimization, user experience (UX), A/B testing, and data analysis to help businesses optimize their landing pages for maximum conversion rates.

11.1 Understanding Landing Page Optimization:

This section introduces the concept of landing page optimization and its significance in digital marketing. It explains how a well-optimized landing page can enhance user experience, increase engagement, and drive higher conversion rates. It discusses the importance of aligning landing page objectives with campaign goals and creating a seamless conversion journey for visitors.

11.2 Defining Clear Conversion Goals:

Defining clear conversion goals is the first step in landing page optimization. This section discusses the importance of setting specific and measurable goals, such as form submissions, purchases, or sign-ups. It emphasizes the need to align these goals with overall business objectives and design landing pages to facilitate the desired actions.

11.3 Optimizing Landing Page Design:

An effective landing page design can significantly impact conversion rates. This section explores design principles and strategies for optimizing landing pages. It discusses elements such as layout, color scheme, typography, imagery, and visual hierarchy. It emphasizes the importance of clean and clutter-free designs that draw attention to key conversion elements.

11.4 Crafting Compelling Copy:

Persuasive copywriting is crucial for engaging visitors and driving conversions on landing pages. This section explores techniques for crafting compelling copy that communicates the value proposition, highlights benefits, and addresses visitor concerns. It discusses the use of persuasive headlines, concise and scannable content, customer testimonials, and compelling storytelling.

11.5 Optimizing Call-to-Action (CTA):

The call-to-action (CTA) is a critical element on a landing page that prompts visitors to take the desired action. This section delves into CTA optimization strategies, including placement, design, wording, and color choices. It explores the importance of clear and compelling CTAs that stand out on the page and create a sense of urgency.

11.6 Enhancing User Experience (UX):

A positive user experience is key to driving conversions on landing pages. This section discusses UX optimization techniques, such as fast page loading times, mobile responsiveness, intuitive navigation, and streamlined forms. It emphasizes the need for user-friendly designs that reduce friction and make it easy for visitors to complete the desired action.

11.7 Conducting A/B Testing:

A/B testing allows businesses to compare different versions of a landing page to identify the most effective elements. This section explores A/B testing strategies, including testing headline variations, CTA button colors, form fields, and layout changes. It discusses the importance of testing one element at a time, gathering sufficient data, and making data-driven decisions for optimization.

11.8 Analyzing Data and Metrics:

Data analysis is essential for understanding the effectiveness of landing pages and identifying areas for improvement. This section discusses key metrics to track, such as conversion rates, bounce rates, time on page, and click-through rates (CTRs). It explores analytics tools and platforms that provide insights into user behavior and help in identifying optimization opportunities.

11.9 Implementing Trust Signals:

Trust signals are elements that instill trust and credibility in visitors, encouraging them to convert. This section explores trust signal strategies, such as customer testimonials, security seals, social proof, and trust badges. It discusses the importance of prominently displaying trust signals on landing pages to alleviate visitor concerns.

11.10 Continual Optimization and Improvement:

Landing page optimization is an ongoing process of continual improvement. This section emphasizes the importance of monitoring performance, analyzing data, and implementing iterative changes to optimize conversion rates. It encourages businesses to stay proactive and make data-driven optimizations based on visitor feedback and evolving market trends.

Conclusion:

This chapter concludes by highlighting the significance of landing page optimization in driving conversions. By focusing on clear conversion goals, optimizing design and copy, refining CTAs, enhancing user experience, conducting A/B testing, analyzing data, and implementing trust signals, businesses can maximize their conversion rates and improve the overall effectiveness of their digital marketing campaigns.

Chapter 12: Harnessing the Potential of Mobile Marketing

Introduction:

Mobile marketing has become an essential component of any successful digital marketing strategy. With the widespread use of smartphones and mobile devices, businesses have the opportunity to reach their target audience anytime, anywhere. This chapter explores the potential of mobile marketing and provides insights into strategies for leveraging this platform effectively. It covers mobile advertising, app marketing, SMS marketing, location-based marketing, and mobile optimization to help businesses harness the power of mobile marketing.

12.1 Understanding the Mobile Marketing Landscape:

This section introduces the concept of mobile marketing and its significance in the digital landscape. It discusses the growth of mobile usage, the shift in consumer behavior towards mobile devices, and the opportunities this presents for businesses. It emphasizes the need for mobile optimization and tailored strategies to engage the mobile audience effectively.

12.2 Mobile Advertising:

Mobile advertising enables businesses to reach their target audience through various mobile channels and platforms. This section explores mobile advertising strategies, including in-app ads, mobile search ads, display ads, and social media ads optimized for mobile devices. It discusses best practices for targeting, ad formats, and optimizing campaigns to maximize engagement and conversions.

12.3 App Marketing:

Mobile apps provide businesses with a unique opportunity to engage users and drive customer loyalty. This section delves into app marketing strategies, including app store optimization (ASO), app reviews and ratings, push notifications, and app deep linking. It discusses the importance of user experience, app performance, and ongoing app promotion to increase app downloads and user engagement.

12.4 SMS Marketing:

SMS marketing allows businesses to reach their audience directly through text messages. This section explores SMS marketing strategies, including opt-in campaigns, personalized messaging, time-sensitive offers, and SMS automation. It discusses compliance with SMS regulations, crafting compelling messages, and measuring the effectiveness of SMS marketing campaigns.

12.5 Location-Based Marketing:

Location-based marketing leverages the mobile device's GPS capabilities to deliver targeted messages and offers based on a user's location. This section explores location-based marketing strategies, including geotargeting, geofencing, and beacon technology. It discusses the benefits of delivering relevant and timely messages to users based on their physical proximity to businesses or specific locations.

12.6 Mobile Optimization:

Mobile optimization is essential to ensure a seamless and engaging user experience on mobile devices. This section discusses the importance of responsive web design, mobile-friendly layouts, fast loading times, and intuitive navigation. It explores techniques for optimizing websites, landing pages, and emails for mobile devices, considering factors such as screen size, touch navigation, and mobile SEO.

12.7 Mobile Customer Engagement:

Mobile marketing offers unique opportunities for customer engagement and interaction. This section explores strategies for mobile customer engagement, including mobile surveys, mobile loyalty programs, interactive mobile ads, and gamification. It discusses the importance of personalization, interactivity, and creating value-added experiences to foster customer loyalty and drive repeat engagement.

12.8 Mobile Analytics and Measurement:

Measuring the effectiveness of mobile marketing efforts is crucial for optimizing strategies and maximizing ROI. This section discusses key mobile marketing metrics, such as app downloads, app engagement, mobile website traffic, and conversion rates. It explores mobile analytics tools and platforms that provide insights into user behavior, preferences, and campaign performance.

12.9 Emerging Trends in Mobile Marketing:

Mobile marketing is an evolving field with emerging trends and technologies. This section highlights current and future trends, such as mobile video marketing, augmented reality (AR), virtual reality (VR), voice search optimization, and mobile wallets. It encourages businesses to stay updated with these trends to stay ahead of the competition and leverage the latest mobile marketing innovations.

Conclusion:

This chapter concludes by emphasizing the vast potential of mobile marketing in reaching and engaging target audiences. By implementing effective mobile advertising, app marketing, SMS marketing, location-based marketing, mobile optimization, and utilizing mobile analytics, businesses can harness the power of mobile marketing to drive brand awareness, customer engagement, and conversions.

Chapter 13: Measuring Campaign Success: Key Metrics and Analytics

Introduction:

Measuring the success of digital marketing campaigns is crucial for optimizing strategies, evaluating ROI, and driving continuous improvement. This chapter explores the key metrics and analytics tools that help businesses assess the performance of their campaigns. It covers tracking website analytics, social media metrics, conversion metrics, customer lifetime value (CLV), return on ad spend (ROAS), and attribution modeling to provide businesses with actionable insights into the effectiveness of their marketing efforts.

13.1 Importance of Measuring Campaign Success:

This section highlights the importance of measuring campaign success in digital marketing. It discusses how data-driven insights enable businesses to make informed decisions, allocate resources effectively, and optimize strategies for better results. It emphasizes the need for defining clear campaign objectives and aligning metrics with these goals.

13.2 Setting Key Performance Indicators (KPIs):

Defining relevant key performance indicators (KPIs) is essential for measuring campaign success. This section explores different KPIs based on campaign objectives, such as website traffic, conversion rates, engagement metrics, customer acquisition cost (CAC), and customer retention rates. It discusses the importance of setting specific, measurable, attainable, relevant, and time-bound (SMART) KPIs.

13.3 Tracking Website Analytics:

Website analytics provide valuable insights into visitor behavior, traffic sources, and conversions. This section explores tracking website analytics using tools like Google Analytics. It discusses metrics such as sessions, bounce rates, average session duration, and conversion funnels. It emphasizes the importance of segmenting data, setting up goals, and using data to optimize website performance.

13.4 Social Media Metrics:

Social media platforms offer a wealth of data that can be used to measure campaign success. This section explores social media metrics such as reach, engagement, follower growth, click-through rates (CTRs), and social media conversions. It discusses the use of social media analytics tools to monitor and analyze campaign performance on platforms like Facebook, Twitter, Instagram, and LinkedIn.

13.5 Conversion Metrics:

Conversion metrics are key indicators of campaign success and ROI. This section delves into conversion metrics, including conversion rates, cost per conversion, and revenue generated. It discusses the importance of tracking conversions across different channels, attributing conversions to specific campaigns, and using conversion data to optimize marketing strategies.

13.6 Customer Lifetime Value (CLV):

Customer lifetime value (CLV) is a metric that quantifies the long-term value of a customer to a business. This section explores CLV calculation methods and discusses how measuring CLV helps businesses understand the profitability of different customer segments. It emphasizes the importance of CLV in customer acquisition and retention strategies.

13.7 Return on Ad Spend (ROAS):

Return on ad spend (ROAS) is a metric that measures the revenue generated from advertising efforts compared to the cost of those ads. This section explores how to calculate ROAS and discusses its significance in assessing the effectiveness of advertising campaigns. It emphasizes the need to track ROAS across different advertising channels and campaigns.

13.8 Attribution Modeling:

Attribution modeling helps businesses understand which marketing channels and touchpoints contribute to conversions. This section explores different attribution models, including first-click attribution, last-click attribution, and multi-touch attribution. It discusses the importance of assigning credit accurately to each touchpoint and using attribution data to optimize marketing budgets and strategies.

13.9 Data Visualization and Reporting:

Data visualization and reporting are essential for effectively communicating campaign performance to stakeholders. This section explores tools and techniques for visualizing data, creating comprehensive reports, and presenting insights in a clear and impactful manner. It discusses the use of dashboards, charts, graphs, and storytelling techniques to convey data-driven narratives.

13.10 Continuous Improvement and Optimization:

Measuring campaign success is an iterative process that requires continuous improvement and optimization. This section emphasizes the importance of ongoing monitoring, analyzing data, and making data-driven adjustments to campaigns. It discusses the concept of agile marketing and the value of A/B testing, experimentation, and learning from insights to optimize future campaigns.

Conclusion:

This chapter concludes by highlighting the significance of measuring campaign success through key metrics and analytics. By tracking website analytics, social media metrics, conversion metrics, CLV, ROAS, and using attribution modeling, businesses can gain valuable insights into their marketing efforts. This data-driven approach enables them to make informed decisions, improve ROI, and drive continuous optimization in their digital marketing campaigns.

Chapter 14: A/B Testing and Optimization Techniques

Introduction:

A/B testing is a powerful technique that allows businesses to optimize their digital marketing efforts by comparing different versions of a webpage, email, or ad to determine the most effective elements. This chapter explores the concept of A/B testing and optimization techniques that help businesses improve conversion rates, user experience, and overall campaign performance. It covers A/B testing best practices, identifying test variables, conducting experiments, analyzing results, and implementing data-driven optimizations.

14.1 Understanding A/B Testing:

This section provides an introduction to A/B testing and its significance in digital marketing. It explains how A/B testing involves creating two or more variations of a marketing element, exposing them to a segmented audience, and analyzing the performance metrics to identify the winning variation. It emphasizes the iterative nature of A/B testing and the role it plays in continuous optimization.

14.2 Setting Clear Testing Objectives:

Defining clear testing objectives is crucial for conducting successful A/B tests. This section explores the importance of aligning testing objectives with campaign goals and identifying specific metrics to measure. It discusses the different objectives that can be tested, such as click-through rates, conversion rates, bounce rates, time on page, and revenue generation.

14.3 Identifying Test Variables:

Identifying the right test variables is essential for obtaining meaningful insights from A/B tests. This section discusses various elements that can be tested, including headlines, call-to-action (CTA) buttons, colors, images, layouts, forms, and messaging. It emphasizes the importance of focusing on one variable at a time to isolate the impact of the tested element.

14.4 Designing A/B Test Experiments:

Designing well-structured A/B test experiments is crucial for accurate and reliable results. This section explores the steps involved in designing A/B tests, including sample size determination, randomization, and control group selection. It discusses the significance of statistical significance and statistical power in ensuring reliable test results.

14.5 Conducting A/B Tests:

This section delves into the practical aspects of conducting A/B tests. It explores various tools and platforms available for setting up and running A/B tests, such as Google Optimize, Optimizely, or custom-built solutions. It discusses the importance of properly implementing the test variations, ensuring consistent user experience, and tracking relevant metrics.

14.6 Analyzing Test Results:

Analyzing test results accurately is crucial for drawing meaningful insights from A/B tests. This section explores techniques for analyzing A/B test data, including statistical analysis, confidence intervals, and hypothesis testing. It discusses the interpretation of test results, identifying winning variations, and understanding the impact of tested elements on the desired metrics.

14.7 Implementing Data-Driven Optimizations:

Implementing data-driven optimizations based on A/B test results is the ultimate goal of A/B testing. This section discusses strategies for implementing successful optimizations, including updating website or app elements, modifying ad campaigns, or refining email marketing strategies. It emphasizes the importance of monitoring post-implementation performance and iteratively improving based on results.

14.8 Multivariate Testing:

Multivariate testing goes beyond A/B testing by simultaneously testing multiple variations of different elements on a webpage or campaign. This section introduces multivariate testing and discusses its benefits, challenges, and considerations. It explores the use of multivariate testing tools and the importance of balancing test complexity with statistical reliability.

14.9 Continuous Optimization and Learning:

A/B testing is an ongoing process of continuous optimization and learning. This section emphasizes the importance of regularly conducting A/B tests, staying updated with industry best practices, and learning from both successful and unsuccessful tests. It discusses the concept of growth mindset and the role of A/B testing in fostering a culture of experimentation and improvement.

Conclusion:

This chapter concludes by highlighting the significance of A/B testing and optimization techniques in improving digital marketing campaigns. By setting clear testing objectives, identifying test variables, conducting experiments, analyzing results, and implementing data-driven optimizations, businesses can enhance conversion rates, user experience, and overall campaign performance.

Chapter 15: Building Long-Term Digital Marketing Strategies

Introduction:

Building a successful long-term digital marketing strategy is essential for sustainable growth and achieving business objectives. This chapter explores the key elements and considerations involved in developing a comprehensive and adaptable digital marketing strategy. It covers market analysis, goal setting, audience targeting, channel selection, content planning, measurement frameworks, and agility to help businesses create strategies that withstand the test of time.

15.1 Market Analysis:

Before building a long-term digital marketing strategy, it is crucial to conduct a thorough market analysis. This section explores the process of market analysis, including assessing industry trends, identifying target markets, understanding customer needs and preferences, and analyzing competitors. It discusses the importance of conducting market research and leveraging data to inform strategy development.

15.2 Defining Goals and Objectives:

Setting clear and measurable goals is a fundamental step in building a long-term digital marketing strategy. This section delves into the process of defining goals and objectives that align with overall business objectives. It discusses the importance of setting SMART goals (specific, measurable, attainable, relevant, and time-bound) and the role they play in guiding strategic decision-making.

15.3 Target Audience Identification:

Identifying and understanding the target audience is essential for effective digital marketing. This section explores techniques for defining target audience segments based on demographics, psychographics, and behavioral factors. It emphasizes the importance of creating buyer personas and leveraging data to develop targeted messaging and personalized experiences.

15.4 Channel Selection and Integration:

Selecting the right digital marketing channels is crucial for reaching and engaging the target audience effectively. This section explores different channels, including search engines, social media platforms, email marketing, content marketing, and influencer marketing. It discusses the importance of aligning channel selection with target audience preferences and campaign goals. It also emphasizes the significance of channel integration for creating cohesive and consistent brand experiences.

15.5 Content Planning and Creation:

Content is at the core of any successful digital marketing strategy. This section explores the process of content planning and creation. It discusses the importance of developing a content strategy, including defining content themes, formats, and distribution channels. It emphasizes the need for high-quality, relevant, and engaging content that resonates with the target audience and aligns with their needs at different stages of the customer journey.

15.6 Measurement and Analytics:

Measurement and analytics are vital for tracking the effectiveness of a long-term digital marketing strategy. This section explores the development of measurement frameworks and the selection of key performance indicators (KPIs) that align with business objectives. It discusses the use of analytics tools and platforms for monitoring and analyzing campaign performance. It also emphasizes the importance of data-driven decision-making and continuous optimization based on insights.

15.7 Agility and Adaptability:

Digital marketing strategies need to be adaptable to changing market dynamics and emerging trends. This section highlights the importance of agility and flexibility in long-term strategies. It discusses the need to monitor and respond to industry shifts, consumer behavior changes, and technological advancements. It emphasizes the iterative nature of digital marketing and the value of learning from data, experimenting with new tactics, and embracing a growth mindset.

15.8 Budgeting and Resource Allocation:

Developing a long-term digital marketing strategy requires careful budgeting and resource allocation. This section explores strategies for budget planning, considering factors such as campaign goals, channel selection, content production, and technology investments. It discusses the importance of allocating resources effectively to maximize the impact of digital marketing initiatives.

15.9 Collaboration and Communication:

Successful long-term digital marketing strategies require collaboration and communication across different teams and stakeholders. This section explores techniques for fostering collaboration, ensuring alignment with other departments (such as sales and customer service), and maintaining consistent messaging and brand identity across channels. It emphasizes the significance of regular communication, feedback loops, and cross-functional teamwork.

Conclusion:

This chapter concludes by emphasizing the importance of building a long-term digital marketing strategy that aligns with business objectives, understands the target audience, leverages the right channels, creates compelling content, measures performance, and embraces adaptability. By incorporating these key elements, businesses can create strategies that drive sustainable growth and achieve long-term success in the digital landscape.

Overall Conclusion

Congratulations! You have reached the end of this comprehensive guide on digital marketing. Throughout this book, we have explored various facets of digital marketing, from understanding the landscape to implementing effective strategies. We have delved into topics like setting objectives, targeting the right audience, crafting compelling content, leveraging different channels, measuring success, and optimizing campaigns.

As you close this book, remember that digital marketing is an ever-evolving field. What works today might not work tomorrow. The digital landscape is constantly changing, presenting new opportunities and challenges. Embrace the dynamic nature of digital marketing and continue to stay curious, innovative, and adaptable.

But knowledge alone is not enough. The true power lies in taking action. It's time to apply what you've learned and embark on your own digital marketing journey. Whether you are a business owner, a marketer, or an aspiring digital marketer, the principles and strategies covered in this book provide a solid foundation for success.

As you move forward, keep these key takeaways in mind:

Strategy is everything: Build your digital marketing efforts on a well-defined strategy aligned with your business objectives. Set clear goals, identify your target audience, and choose the right channels and tactics to reach them effectively.

Data is your compass: Leverage data and analytics to gain insights into your audience, measure performance, and make data-driven decisions. Continuously monitor and optimize your campaigns based on the feedback provided by the data.

Content is king: Create compelling, valuable, and relevant content that resonates with your audience. Develop a content strategy that addresses their needs, guides them through the buyer's journey, and fosters long-term relationships.

Adaptability is key: Stay agile and adaptable in the face of changing trends and technologies. Embrace experimentation, learn from failures, and continuously evolve your strategies to stay ahead of the competition.

Collaboration breeds success: Foster collaboration and communication within your team and across departments. Digital marketing is a multidisciplinary field, and collaboration can lead to innovative ideas, streamlined processes, and better results.

Remember, digital marketing is not a destination; it's a journey. Embrace the excitement of constant learning, experimentation, and growth. Stay curious, seek new knowledge, and keep up with industry trends. The world of digital marketing is filled with opportunities waiting to be explored.

Now, it's time to take what you've learned and make an impact. Implement the strategies, adapt them to your unique circumstances, and don't be afraid to think outside the box. Your journey in digital marketing has just begun, and the possibilities are limitless.

Thank you for joining us on this enlightening journey. We wish you success in all your digital marketing endeavors. Remember, the future is digital, and it's yours to conquer!

Best of luck,

By
   Naitik Sharma & Nilesh Sharma